D0276644

FEBRUARY

S	M	T	W	T	F	S
	1	2	3	4	5	6
7	8	9	10	11	12	13
14	15	16	17	18	19	20
21	22	23	24	25	26	27
28						

APRIL

S	M	T	W	T	F	S
				1	2	3
4	5	6	7	8	9	10
11	12	13	14	15	16	17
18	19	20	21	22	23	24
25	26	27	28	29	30	

HAPPY EA

HAPPY EASTER

EASTER

JUNE

S	M	T	W	T	F	S
		1	2	3	4	5
6	7	8	9	10	11	12
13	14	15	16	17	18	19
20	21	22	23	24	25	26
27	28	29	30			

CONTENTS

The Fireside Book

A picture and a poem
for every mood
chosen by

David Hope

Printed and published by
D.C. THOMSON & CO., LTD.,
185 Fleet Street, LONDON EC4A 2HS.
© D.C. Thomson & Co., Ltd., 1998.
ISBN 0-85116-670-9

WINTER WHITE

THE fragile wisps of icy snow
Come dancing down the breeze,
To settle on the chimney-pots
On rooftops and on eaves.
The garden clad in Winter white
Takes on an eerie glow,
And trees with boughs like outstretched arms
Are laden down with snow.

Like feathers drifting silently
And floating through the night,
The glistening snowflakes hide the world
Beneath a veil of white.
It almost seems like fairyland
With gems on every tree,
Just looking through my window pane
A magic world I see.

Kathleen Gillum

THE SLIDE

WE longed for the sharp crinkle of December stars,
   That ghostly mist like cobwebs in the grass —
Ten degrees below zero.

After the snow came petalling from the skies,
Settled into a deep quilt, the frost
Diamonded the top, making a thick crust.

On the long descent of the lawn
We made our slide, planed the ground
Hour after hour till it smiled with ice.

At night we teetered out with buckets,
Rushed the water down the slide's length
In one black stain.

Next day the slide was lethal,
A curling glacier that shot us downhill
In a single hiss.

Even after the thaw greened our world again
The slide remained written in the grass
As long as our stories.

Kenneth C. Steven

TO GRANDCHILDREN

THOUGH Winter's frosty fingers
   Have touched my heart with rime,
In your sweet, flower faces
I glimpse my Summertime.

I am a tree, a weathered oak
Bowed by Winter pain,
Through you, my dewy, flowering buds
My leaves are green again.

To the faded garden of my years
Fresh, tender bloom you bring,
Awake the birds, their joyful cries,
Glad echoes of my Spring!

Eileen Melrose.

GOD'S GIFTS

I LOOKED at the sky
  In the morning's light
Burnished rose, gold,
Reflecting God's might.

I looked at the earth,
Under a blanket of snow.
Glittering white crystals,
Reflecting the glow.

I looked at the trees,
Heavy with frost.
Black limbs pointing,
Reflecting life lost.

I looked at the mountains,
Through the eyes of a man.
Majestically forbidding,
Reflecting God's plan.

I looked in myself,
Finding strength to cope.
Discovering belief,
Reflecting my hope.

I looked at the sky,
Through different eyes.
Reflecting my faith,
Thank God I'm alive . . .

Morag McCluskey

FIRST WARM DAY

FIELD edges intricate with grace
  Of Lady Anne's exquisite lace,
Dandelion clocks half blown
Beside these clay fields safely sown
And in this month of little dark
The lengthy singing of the lark.

In mustard yellow fields of rape
The roe deer makes a shy escape
To drop her dappled, pristine fawn
Fear of invasion almost gone
Close, bearded-barley fields of green
Ripple in miles of crêpe-de-chine.

I wander underneath a sky
Pierced by an oystercatcher's cry.
Back home, by thrush from farmhouse
  lawn
A most reluctant worm is drawn
While blackbird solo, wild and free,
Rings from the turret of a tree . . .

From outer pathways that we stroll
Come inner wanderings of the soul.
Margaret Gillies Brown

WHAT IS A HOME?

A SPECIAL place that warms the heart
   Where love and peace both play their part,
A shelter where we run and hide,
A refuge from the world outside.
A home is filled with plans and schemes,
With memories and precious dreams,
A house, a flat, a caravan,
A castle, fit for everyman.
And though we travel, far and wide,
Our home is where our hearts reside,
And so, once more, our steps will lead
Back home, the only place we need!

Iris Hesselden

THE PLAYROOM

OF all the rooms in Manor House
   The playroom was the best;
For years abandoned and silent,
There our cherished toys rest.

Gone is our boisterous childhood
When we, as girls and boys,
Played happily for hours on end
With magic, lifelike toys.

A fort with leaden soldiers,
A clockwork railway set,
Reminders of a bygone age —
Could ever I forget?

Neglected are the rocking-horse
And well-equipped doll's house,
Covered with cobwebs, grime and dust,
Disturbed by moth and mouse.

The room is an Aladdin's Cave —
A children's paradise;
Today, for such old-fashioned toys
Collectors pay top price.

But very soon, I much regret,
These toys of yesteryear
By public auction will be sold
And, sadly, disappear.

Glynfab John

THE THRUSH'S NEST

WITHIN a thick and spreading hawthorn bush
    That overhung a mole-hill large and round,
I heard from morn to morn a merry thrush
Sing hymns to sunrise, while I drank the sound
With joy; and, often an intruding guest,
I watched her secret toils from day to day —
How true she warped the moss to form a nest,
And modelled it within with wood and clay;
And by and by, like heath-bells gilt with dew,
There lay her shining eggs, as bright as flowers,
Ink-spotted over shells of greeny blue;
And there I witnessed, in the sunny hours,
A brood of nature's minstrels chirp and fly,
Glad as that sunshine and the laughing sky.

John Clare

THE EARTHWORM

HELPLESS you writhe in your despair
  When, all unwitting, I lay bare
Your refuge in the dank and fragrant earth.

Am I alone in hastening to seek
To re-inter you in the soil,
Protect you from the thrush and blackbird's beak?

For I, who share the satisfying joy
Which Adam knew, in honest toil
With spade and rake and hoe,

Am full aware that not a blade would grow
Without your lowly presence, in the end,
Small earthworm, gardeners' friend.

Roseleen N. Milne

BEE-HAVIOUR

APRIL —
   And an early plunderer
Is out among the flowers.
Wallflower warms the air.
He enters velvet caves,
Collecting contraband,
Watched by the old stone head
Made featureless by storms.

With drowsy hum
The smuggler-bee moves on
Distributing gold dust
Quite unaware of pattern
Or of purpose . . .

Unconscious of cog status
On earth's gigantic wheel.

Margaret Gillies Brown

THE LONELY BEACH

THIS solitary stretch of beach
  Is so remote and out of reach
No children ever laugh and play,
And footprints are a rarity.
Upon this burnished sweep of sand
No bouncing beach-balls ever land,
Or sleepy folk in deck-chairs snore
Or donkeys trot along the shore,
And on these silky golden grains
You'll find no picnicker's remains —
Yet there are some who patronise
This spot, and swooping from the skies
To paddle long-legged in the sea
And seek out shell-fish for their tea,
Once again these hungry waders
Are the beach's sole invaders.

Alison Mary Fitt

OUT WITH GRANDMA

WHEN me and Grandma take a walk
  Both hand in hand, together,
She never tries to hurry me
Or worries 'bout the weather.
We count the cars, so many cars,
Ten red, five blue, one green
And then the vans and lorries
The biggest ever seen!

We find a pool and throw some stones,
So I can hear them plop,
And then we change the traffic lights
And all the buses stop!
When we get back, my mummy says,
"Why are your shoes so dirty?"
Sometimes I think she's getting old,
'Cos Grandma's nearly thirty!

When Grandma leaves, she pats my head,
She knows I'm sick of kissing,
Next week we'll have another walk
And see what we've been missing!

Iris Hesselden

MY DARLING

LAST night the nightingale woke me
  Last night when all was still
It sang in the golden moonlight
From out the woodland hill
It sang of love and beauty
Of a heart that still was true
And oh, the bird, my darling, was singing
Was singing of you, of you.

I think of you in the daytime
I dream of you by night
I wake, and wish you were here, love
And tears are blinding my sight
I hear a low breath in the lime tree
The wind is floating through
And oh, the night, my darling, is sighing
Is sighing for you, for you.

I think not I can forget you
I could not though I would
I see you in all around me
The stream, the night, the wood
The flowers that slumber so gently
The stars above so blue
And heaven itself my darling, is praying
Is praying for you, for you.

William Prentice

OVER THE
GARDEN WALL

REMEMBER when we used to peep
Over the garden wall,
Standing upon an orange-box
Because we were so small?

Remember how I tried to climb
Over the garden wall,
To play games on the other side,
And had a nasty fall?

Remember how you loved to tease
Over the garden wall,
Yet I remained your closest friend,
And gave you my new ball?

Remember how we dared to kiss
Over the garden wall,
Quite certain we could not be seen,
But heard my mother call?

Remember how we said goodbye
Over the garden wall,
When tearfully you moved away,
And left me once for all?

You still remember? So do I!
But we are now grown tall,
And we no longer both have fun
Over the garden wall.

Glynfab John

BELINDA AND I

WE saw the kingfisher,
  Belinda and I,
Down by the steam where the brown trout lie.
A swift flash of blue —
Now here, now gone!
Leaving Belinda and me quite alone.

A sombre grey heron
Stood quietly by
Where we hid in the reeds, Belinda and I:
Bright yellow flag iris
And kingcups grew there
Beside Ragged Robin and windflowers fair.

There were dragonflies, too
And a little brown otter
A-swim on his back, making rings in the water,
And I can remember that
Nearby there stood
A willow with catkins and satin-smooth wood.

I guess I'd been six, then,
While she'd been but three!
Now soon we'll be wedded . . .
Belinda and Me.

Mary M. Milne

SUMMER'S SYMBOL

SUMMER'S beauty captured
  By the essence of the rose,
Symbol of the season,
Whose haunting fragrance shows
A promise of enchantment,
Filling every breath of air,
Within this perfect day ahead
For everyone to share!
Bud of early morning
Drenched in the sheen of dew,
Or blossomed out in splendour
Of its lovely, varied hue,
The rose is always special,
And very much a part
Of the hopes that in its blossom,
Are inspired through every heart!

Elizabeth Gozney

BUTTERFLY

A SILKEN shape with flimsy wings
And fairylike in form,
I watch you dart and dance your way
Across the garden lawn.
A perfect thing quite beautiful
Fluttering in the sun,
Sipping nectar from the blooms
You visit one by one.

Your colours are so delicate
In tones and tints of blue,
Hovering amongst the flowers
Of every shade and hue.
Elusive little butterfly
Enjoying sunny days,
I'm lost in captive wonder as
You hold my steady gaze.

You come and settle by my hand
And I reach out to you,
I try to touch your fragile wings
Of velvet powder blue —
But off you soar upon the breeze
Into the Summer sky,
You're one of Nature's precious gems —
Exquisite butterfly.

Kathleen Gillum

GATHERING

CATCHING the ear
    With a murmur like bees,
Bleat upon bleat
And hundred upon hundred,
Gathered by unseen men
And dogs across the water.

Heavy-bellied clouds
Sag in the warm air.
An amiable wind
Rags the bog-cotton
Water grey and wrinkled,
Shining between islands.
Murmur of distant sheep
Like bees.

Ian Dubh

THE STOLEN ROSE

WHERE have you gone, my lovely fragrant rose?
Last night I watched your petals softly close.
Have you been borne upon the Summer breeze
That murmured in the night among the trees?
Or did you come within a vandal's grasp
Who rudely plucked you as he passed?
Or was it an admirer going by
Who thought he loved you more than I?

This morn, where'er you find repose,
Farewell, farewell, my lovely rose!

There will be other blooms upon your branch;
They'll stay to charm me, longer than you did,
   perchance;
You were my first, my crimson bloom,
Flourishing — though to leave me soon!
Do you delight another's eye,
Or in some dark, forgotten corner lie?
You gave me joy — upon majestic stem
Lovelier — far lovelier — than the costliest gem!

Again, where'er you find repose,
Farewell, farewell, my lovely rose!

Patricia McGavock

SUMMER LAMENT

I LOVE the lazy Summer days
With nothing much to do.
But lift the bulbs and mow the grass.
And feed the roses, too.
And stake the drooping dahlias,
And trim along the hedge,
And chase the greenfly off the blooms
And harvest all the veg.
And spray against the dreaded blight,
And prune around the shrubs,
And save some seeds, and kill the weeds
And water all the tubs.
Oh, how I love the Summer days,
And yet of this I'm sure:
I shall not grieve to see them leave,
And Winter comes once more!

Margaret Ingall

HALLOWED MEMORIES

IT stands, just at the village edge,
  An ancient building, small and grey,
With glinting spire above the hedge,
And clock, to chime the hours away.

Within the gentle shade of trees,
Where swallows nest and breezes sigh,
They rest, in peace of centuries,
Who lived, and loved, in days gone by.

But happier thoughts come, vivid still,
Of bridal whiteness, music, flowers,
And christenings when, with right good will,
We brought those lovely babes of ours.

Though years have passed and, like most folk
We've lived our lives in other places,
What memories those walls evoke
Of youth, and love, and children's faces!

That's why, when passing on the bus,
For one more glimpse I turn my head.
It's always meant so much to us —
That little church, where we were wed . . .

Kathleen O'Farrell

NIGHT LIFE

MOTH — drawn through my open window
From fluttering darkness
By this irresistible lamp;
Palest cinnamon, you lie for a moment
Stretched out on my green cover,
Make a delicate motif.

No agile-woman-hand
Could weave so finely
The symmetry of pattern
Woven in your wings.

What will you do
When I turn off the light?
Return to the summer stars
And moon glow?

Margaret Gillies Brown

A SONG FOR SUMMER

ALONE beside the singing stream
I watch a cloud above a hill.
Another day! Another dream!
And free to wander where I will.

Afar, where tide and heavens meet,
The gulls are crying o'er the bay;
And here the breeze sighs to the wheat:
How swiftly Summer slips away.

Deep in the woods at hush of noon,
I drink the waters of the brook.
Why weep that youth must pass so soon?
Why yearn to read the future's book?

Then sunset's glory paints the west,
And dusk begins her shadow-play.
Even a wanderer must rest:
Farewell! Farewell! Sweet Summer day.

Peter Cliffe

ANCESTRAL HOME

OLD stone walls that time has mellowed
Grace this lovely home,
Enveloping the gardens in
A beauty of their own.
Tall majestic cedar trees
Have braved the wind and rain,
While peacocks strutting on the lawn
Seem elegant and vain.
Timbered beams and old oak panels
Which were built to last,
Just seem to me to conjure up
The spirit of the past.

The many armoured knights of old,
Each painting and antique,
And varied wondrous works of art
Priceless and unique.
It's here the beauty lovers meet
To come and feast their eyes,
Upon the relics of the past —
History never dies.
A beautiful ancestral home
Standing on a hill,
One feels in such a place as this
That time is standing still.

Kathleen Gillum

OUR GARDEN SWING

DANGLING from the apple tree
In Winter's cold and Summer's heat
Our garden swing, once pushed by me
Has long time had an empty seat.

The only occupants you'd see
Were birds, perched swaying to and fro,
While in the winter it would be
Motionless, immersed in snow.

For since my children clambered on
The seat, to soar aloft each day
To giddy heights, the years have gone,
They've all grown up and gone away.

But now a cry of "Push me high!"
Is heard from my young grandson, Ben —
I'm glad to say the swing and I
Are back in business once again!

Alison Mary Fitt

MEG MERRILEES

OLD Meg she was a gipsy,
  And lived upon the moors;
Her bed it was the brown heath turf,
And her house was out of doors,
Her apples were swart blackberries,
Her currants, pods o' broom;
Her wine was dew of the wild white rose,
Her book a churchyard tomb.

Her brothers were the craggy hills,
Her sisters larchen trees;
Alone with her great family
She lived as she did please.
No breakfast had she many a morn,
No dinner many a noon,
And, 'stead of supper, she would stare
Full hard against the moon.

But every morn, of woodbine fresh,
She made her garlanding,
And, every night, the dark glen yew
She wove, and she would sing.
And with her fingers, old and brown,
She plaited mats of rushes,
And gave them to the cottagers
She met among the bushes.

Old Meg was brave as Margaret Queen,
And tall as Amazon;
An old red blanket cloak she wore,
A chip-hat had she on:
God rest her aged bones somewhere!
She died full long agone!

John Keats

SEASON OF DELIGHT

SUMMER is opening her door,
And through it one sees
Lavender, lilies, and lupins,
A-quiver with bees;
Hollyhocks, under old thatch,
And butterfly wings outspread
On ancient, honey-coloured walls,
Mid roses, yellow and red.

Summer is opening her door,
And a glimmer comes through
Of little white sails that dip and sway
On a sea of sparkling blue;
Where barefoot children run,
With buckets and spades in hand,
In a dazzle of fluttering gulls,
And shimmering sand.

Summer is opening her door,
New delights to unfold,
And bids us enter her lovely realm
Of crystal, sapphire and gold.

Kathleen O'Farrell

STEPPING STONES

I PONDERED briefly, at a loss,
  Should I leap or should I wade?
Then I saw them neatly laid
Side by side, for me to cross.

Who put them there? The water's flow
Was wandering wetly round about
As gratefully I ventured out,
I don't suppose I'll ever know.

Perhaps some civil engineer
Now building bridges far away
Once laid them, as a lad at play
In practice for his life's career.

Or maybe weary campers bent
On crossing over to a site
To put their tent up for a night,
Or thoughtful country resident.

But I can only guess and thank
Whoever did, I won't forget
They kept my feet from getting wet
As I approached the other bank.

And thank you, too, to friends who seem
To be there with a caring deed
And warming word in times of need,
Like stepping stones across a stream.

Alison Mary Fitt

FIRESIDE SONG

I SIT beside the fire and think
  Of places long ago,
Of feeding ducks beside a lake
And Winter walks in snow.
Of how the morning sun arose
Beyond the distant hill,
And life was all excitement then,
Sometimes, I feel it still.
I sit beside the fire at night
As winds blow round the eaves,
And I remember Autumn days,
The crunch of golden leaves.
I sit and think of bluebell woods
Where trees met overhead,
And as the pathway wandered on
We followed where it led.
I sit beside the fire and think
Of those I used to know,
And I remember happy times
And places long ago.

Iris Hesselden

OLD COUNTRY ROSES

AGAINST the rustic porch they climb
And round the cottage door,
Cascading down the cream-washed walls
They trail across the floor.
Their colours which are beautiful
Are scarlet, pink and flame,
Each rose so individual
Alike but not the same.

Their beauty seems to touch my heart
With perfume fine and sweet,
As velvet petals with the breeze
Lie scattered at my feet.
The tumbling roses bend and sway
Against the garden wall,
And subtle fragrance fills the air
As twilight starts to fall.

Reflecting on their loveliness
Old thoughts come stealing in,
Rekindling thoughts of days now past
And memories within.
As I look back remembering
My childhood days once more,
I see old country roses cling
And cluster round the door.

Kathleen Gillum

ROSE COTTAGE

THE ROW

THERE is a kettle on the range
   With its lid rattling and foaming —
The kitchen smells of butter and new meat.
The dog lies fanned out on the floor,
Mild eyes the colour of whisky, watching
Me shivering on an ancient chair,
My hair hedgehogged and shining with water,
Ten years old, having fallen in a bog.

Outside the night has come down
Like tar. There is only one rickety lane
Riding away west, and that has been swallowed.
All has slid into dark, except a few flint bits of star
That spark the skies.

And I am shivering on the kitchen chair,
Watching the mellow blinking of the collie's eyes,
Ten years old, waiting for the row.

Kenneth C. Steven

THE KITTEN AT PLAY

SEE the kitten on the wall,
  Sporting with the leaves that fall,
Withered leaves, one, two and three,
Falling from the elder-tree;
Through the calm and frosty air
Of the morning bright and fair.

See the kitten, how she starts,
Crouches, stretches, paws and darts;
With a tiger-leap half way
Now she meets her coming prey.
Lets it go as fast as then
Has it in her power again.

Now she works with three and four,
Like an Indian conjurer;
Quick as he in feats of art,
Gracefully she plays her part;
Yet were gazing thousands there,
What would little Tabby care?

William Wordsworth

POINT OF DEPARTURE

STRANGER, with the loaded rucksack,
  Clearly labelled "Kinlochewe",
How I wish this glorious May-morn
I were coming with you, too.

Ponder all that lies before you,
As on your way you sally forth,
And the track beyond horizon
Leads you ever farther north.

Overnighting then near Moffat
Yonder side of Beattock Pass
Where the moorland breeze goes singing
Through the pine trees and the grass.

Wild tormentil, sparkling eyebright,
Lady's smock (or cardamine)
Ferns and rushes by the water,
Primroses and celandine.

You'll wander in Elysian fields
And in blue remembered hills.
Oh what dreams, oh what heartache
Each glorious name my memory fills.

There's The Saddle and An Teallach,
Sgurr Alasdair, Beinn Alligin,
Sgurr Fiona, Slioch, Tolmount,
Two Ben Vorlichs, proud In Pin.

Every incline, every turning
Count them off upon your hand.
Every mile is one mile nearer
To the magic promised land.

Think of sunrise over Kintail
And sunset over Wester Ross.
Smell of peat evokes such longing
For misty moors we all must cross.

Map and compass at the ready;
You just can't wait for journey's end!
Good luck, good health, may joy be with you
Happy Munro-bagging, friend!

Ann Griffiths

SERENITY . . .

THE glorious rays of setting sun
Throw sharply in relief,
The stillness of the tawny owl,
A sighting — all too brief!
Then drifting by horizon's rim,
Thus fades the final ray,
And darkness makes its swift descent
To blot all trace of day!
The tawny owl is stirring now,
And silently swoops by,
Intent upon nocturnal haunts
With sudden, hooting cry!
The myriad stars on velvet black,
Though distant orbs of light —
Now add enchantment to the scene,
And beauty to the night . . .

Elizabeth Gozney

LULLABY

AS evening draws her cloak of grey
   Across the golden sky,
I'll rock your cradle to and fro
And sing a lullaby —
Of soft green leaves and butterflies
And birds with tinted wings —
Of flowers with velvet faces
And lots of pretty things.
And as stars twinkle in the sky
I'll kiss your curly head,
And when you close your sleepy eyes
I'll tuck you in your bed.

Kathleen Gillum

WELCOME TO AUTUMN

THE heather has faded, the summer is over,
Farewell to the harebell, the daisy, the clover,
Farewell to the days when we lazed in the sun,
The season of beauty — so lately begun.
Now welcome to Autumn and fireside pleasure,
To friendship rekindled and evenings to treasure,
The trees turning golden and mist on the fell,
Of warm thoughts to cherish and stories to tell.
So don't be downhearted, be cheerful in mind,
If Winter comes shortly — is Spring far behind?

Iris Hesselden

SOLITUDE

WILLOW, old willow, bend down to the stream;
  Here where your shadow falls, here let me dream,
While the red Autumn sun dies in the west;
By the sweet evening breeze gently caressed.

Laura is far away, gone to the town,
Lissom and auburn-haired, in her green gown.
Think of me, pray for me, while we're apart,
Girl of the winning smile, queen of my heart.

Homeward, turn homeward, for shadows grow long,
Cold is the night wind now; hear its sad song.
High in a cloudless sky bright stars I see,
Watching, aye, watching, o'er Laura and me.

Peter Cliffe

DAUGHTER'S WEDDING

IT'S here at last, your wedding day
  You soon will be a bride,
Today you'll leave this little church
With husband by your side.
Just reminiscing, looking back
As I stand in the pew,
The time has flown so quickly
Where have the years gone to?

I turn to see my little girl
Come walking up the aisle,
Leaning on her father's arm,
Her face a beaming smile.
Her eyes are filled with tenderness
And mine are filled with tears,
As I look back on childhood days
And then to teenage years.

We've had so many lovely times,
We've shared so many things,
Thoughts, ambitions, dreams, desires,
And hopes that soared on wings,
But now I have to let you go —
My thoughts are in a whirl —
This lovely radiant woman
Is still my little girl.

Kathleen Gillum

AUTUMN ROSES

FROM the chilled buds
A curling of dusky petals;
Fragile as promises,
Wistful as heartache.
A tearfall of velvet dust
Stirring the drowsy earth
With October's dying breath.
Despite the soft rain of petals,
The leaves still glowing green,
The thorns still sharp as unrequited hope.

Joan Howes

SEASONS OF LOVE

I LOVED her in the Springtime
   When buds on bare boughs burst,
And in the lanes courted her
As often as I durst.

I loved her in the Summer
When green-clad were the trees,
And the fragrance of wild flowers
Was borne upon the breeze.

I loved her in the Autumn
When leaves began to fall,
And woods bedight with colours
Held both of us in thrall.

I love her still in Winter
When days are bleakly grey,
And through life's changing seasons
Together, close, we stay.

Glynfab John

THE WINDOW SEAT

I SIT by the window and look at the sky
   When strong winds are blowing and clouds racing by,
And up go my thoughts, like a kite on the breeze,
Away 'cross the chimneys and over the trees.

I sit by the window and look at the sky
When clouds are like cotton-wool, fleecy and high,
And I think of the Summertime, long years ago,
The paths through the woodland we all used to know,
The fun and the laughter, so easy to find,
And other warm memories still left behind.

I sit by the window and look at the sky
As daytime grows weary and evening is nigh,
And soon, in the twilight, the first star appears,
And there's peace in my heart as I turn back the years.

Iris Hesselden

DUMBARTON ROCK IN RAIN

FLURRIES of watery spears from the west
   Blur the massy vertical buttresses.
Summer's green cascades the black-brow'd rocks,
Chenille of briar, velvet of grass.
Lupins, foxgloves, nodding in crannies
The sparsest of embroidery.
Hawthorn bobbles roughen the eastern outline.
Man's handstitching of railing
Atop pale patchwork of castle wall,
Wheeling seagulls a wild mobile.

Joe H. McGibbon

LEISURE

A CHAIR beside the fire
  The bright flames leaping
A window and a door
With hinges creaking.

A book I love to read
Its pages turning
I stoke the fire a bit,
To help its burning.

A sense of solitude
With no endeavour
Save reading once again
A tale I treasure.

A lovely sense of peace
My eyes are closing
My book makes no sense now
I must be dozing.

The book — the warmth —
  the fire —
I have most perfect measure
Of that delightful space
That people know — as LEISURE.

Margaret Dixon

FROSTY MORNING

A SUDDEN nip is in the air
But beauty in the day,
And everything seems crisp and chill
For Winter's on its way.
There's frost upon the rustic porch
And ice curls on the pond,
The grass stands out like frozen spears
Transformed by Winter's wand.

And spider webs of jewelled silk
On tinselled twig and tree,
Resemble shawls of dainty lace
In sparkling filigree.
The frost is spread like silver dust
That's sprinkled on the ground,
And crystal beads of icy gems
Lie glinting all around.

And right across the garden fence
Etched out in silvery rime,
A thousand glistening shapes have formed
A shimmering design.
The garden looks so beautiful
At this time of the year,
On this lovely frosty morn
When Winter's almost here.

Kathleen Gillum

SNOW BLANKETS

THE wind has dropped. No frost last night,
  And now, today, the world is white.
The snow has clothed the walls and trees,
And spread her blankets out with ease.
The birds are silent. Nothing stirs,
Save, by the fire, the tabby purrs.
The distant hills blend with the sky,
As time ticks softly, slowly by.
And so we watch and think of Spring,
As white snow blankets everything.

Iris Hesselden

SKATERS ON THE POND

THE sky is clear, the moon shines bright,
The frosty air is keen tonight;
Transformed by Nature is the pond
When Winter waves its magic wand,
And now deep-frozen, solid ice,
It is a prospect to entice
Folk to put on skates, and thrill to glide
Around the pond, aglow with pride;
Thick is the ice that bears the weight
Of those who here just love to skate.

The lanterns shed their mellow light
Upon the cheerful New Year sight;
Muffled up, wearing scarves and gloves,
Young men waltz with their lady-loves:
Confident partners both move as one,
Skilful, graceful, and full of fun,
Flashing by with apparent ease,
Skirting the verges, under the trees,
Over a surface, smooth and white —
Epitome of sheer delight.

Glynfab John

SNOWFALL NEAR
THE OCHILS

I LOVE days
  When snow blankets the fields
And a white mantle descends
Laying a covering
On hedge and tree.
When darkness falls
An opaque whiteness still
Lightens fields and byways
Long after day is done.
Soon I am taken into a fold
Of night and become
Unseen, unknown,
In a silent partnership.

Patrick Clarke

WINTER MAGIC

KING WINTER in his tinselled robes
   Arrived in depth of night,
Transforming all the sleeping town
Into a scene of white.
He came as if on slippered feet
When all was quiet and still,
And blowing with his icy breath
The air turned crisp and chill.
The trees stood out in silhouette
Like frozen sentinels,
With dangling orbs and icicles
That gleamed like crystal bells.

The woods seemed bathed in pearly light
With opalescent glow,
And glinting gems of glistening rime
Were sparkling in the snow.
On every hedge and shrub and bush
In garden, field and park,
A shimmering of shining shapes
Were glittering in the dark.
And in the silvery silent hours
When snowflakes start to fall,
King Winter hides a slumbering world
Beneath a lacy shawl.

Kathleen Gillum

NEW YEAR

THE first of January is here
   And warmly, up and down the land
We raise a glass, and grip a hand,
And wish for all a good new year.

With cheerful smile we toast the new,
New calendars upon the wall
New resolutions made by all,
And yet we're apprehensive, too.

What will the coming twelve months hold?
They are as yet an unwalked mile,
An unsung song, an uncrossed stile,
A story that's as yet untold.

But let us everyone take heart,
The failures of the year just gone
Are all behind, and we are on
The threshold of a brand-new start.

And may we resolutely set
Our sails on this uncharted sea —
Who knows, my friend, for you and me
This may be the best year yet!

Alison Mary Fitt

FROST

THE first frost quickly petrified
And immobilised the countryside,
Tender plants, their life suspended,
The season's leaf and flower ended.

Sprinkled with white frozen dust,
Paralysed by nature's thrust;
Dew no longer there to sip,
Tranquil in an icy grip.

Spiders' webs immortalised,
In spiral wheels solidified.
Held in Winter's steel-like hold,
So fascinating to behold.

Nature's icing on her cake,
A task no man could undertake;
And so her muted song she'll sing
Until released by next year's Spring.

Brian Gent

The artists are: —

Sheila Carmichael; God's Gifts, My Darling, Seasons Of Love

Jackie Cartwright; Belinda And I, Point Of Departure

John Dugan; First Warm Day, Butterfly, The Stolen Rose, Meg Merrilees, Solitude

Danny Ferguson; Ancestral Home

Alan Haldane; Summer's Symbol, Summer Lament, A Song For Summer, Frosty Morning

Eunice Harvey; To Grandchildren, Bee-Haviour, The Kitten At Play, Serenity . . .

Harry McGregor; Season Of Delight, Fireside Song, Snowfall Near The Ochils

John Mackay; Leisure, New Year

Sandy Milligan; Winter White, The Row, Lullaby, Skaters On The Pond

Keith Robson; What Is A Home?, Hallowed Memories, Dumbarton Rock In Rain, Winter Magic

Staff Artists; The Slide, The Playroom, The Thrush's Nest, The Earthworm, The Lonely Beach, Out With Grandma, Over The Garden Wall, Gathering, Night Life, Our Garden Swing, Stepping Stones, Old Country Roses, Welcome To Autumn, Daughter's Wedding, Autumn Roses, The Window Seat, Snow Blankets, Frost

JULY

S	M	T	W	T	F	S
				1	2	3
4	5	6	7	8	9	10
11	12	13	14	15	16	17
18	19	20	21	22	23	24
25	26	27	28	29	30	31

SEPTEMBER

S	M	T	W	T	F	S
			1	2	3	4
5	6	7	8	9	10	11
12	13	14	15	16	17	18
19	20	21	22	23	24	25
26	27	28	29	30		

NOVEMBER

S	M	T	W	T	F	S
	1	2	3	4	5	6
7	8	9	10	11	12	13
14	15	16	17	18	19	20
21	22	23	24	25	26	27
28	29	30				